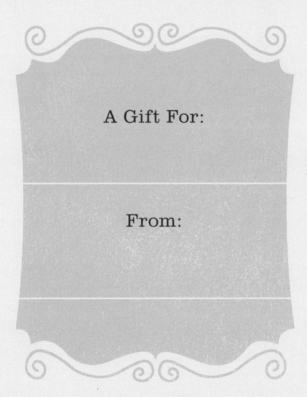

A Gift For:

From:

Writer and Editor: Chelsea Fogleman
Art Director: Kevin Swanson
Designer: Mary Eakin
Production Artist: Dan Horton

ISBN: 978-1-59530-338-7
BOK3114

Printed and bound in China

THE GIFT OF
Shopping Your Style

GIFT BOOKS

THE GIFT OF
Shopping Your Style

Hello,
Fabulous!

$\mathcal{E}$ver feel the urge to splurge?
Maybe you find yourself sighing,
"Oh, I can't justify buying that..."

But aha! That's where you're wrong.
This time, you can justify splurging.

Because you are receiving full permission
to release your inner diva*.

* (Pssst . . . That means you get to go somewhere,
pick out exactly what you want, and you don't have
to compromise with anybody!)

Of course, when it comes to shopping, you've got lots of options.

So let's start by looking at some of the top
shopping contenders.

Shopping for . . .
Clothes

You've got style. Now it's time to work it!

. . . .

What can't you resist?

- The blouse that makes your skin glow?

- The cardigan that says "fun" and "sophisticated" at the same time?

- The jeans that accentuate what you've got going on?

The old saying is true:
"It's what's inside that counts."

Still, there's nothing wrong with dolling
up your outside if you want!

If anyone questions your need for clothing,
you tell that person, "Fashion is art, and
I am an artist.* I just happen to have found
a marvelous canvas in myself."

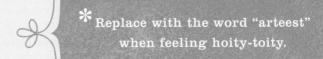

*Replace with the word "arteest"
when feeling hoity-toity.

Shoes

The key to long-term happy feet is proper strategizing.

. . . .

Thankfully, these days, you don't always have to choose between style and comfort. There are lots of cute flats that let your footwear scream "fashionable" while your toes still feel happy.

Sadly though, even in this modern era, women are sometimes faced with a difficult choice: Style or Comfort? Which should rule?

When you're at a loss as to which shoe to go with, you may find this chart helpful:

	Go for style (high heels)	Go for comfort (flats)
Sitting at a desk all day	X	
Standing for more than 30% of your day		X
Walking briskly or for more than a few minutes		X
Attending formal gatherings	X	
Standing before a group for a presentation	X	
Being in any place where no one can see your feet		X

 ✱ Diva Pointer: If you've got a roomy handbag, you can always carry an extra pair of shoes with you. Then you can alternate between "comfort" and "style" as necessary.

Shopping for . . .

Accessories

The right accessories can give any outfit a touch of "ooh la la!"

. . . .

You've got options galore, too . . .

necklace

bag

ring

belt

earrings

sunglasses

purse

scarf

bracelet

clutch

watch

anklet

Diva Pointer: If you have a few versatile accessories in your closet, you can make a small number of tops and bottoms seem like a gazillion different outfits—one day wearing your favorite sweater with a necklace, next time pairing it with a pretty belt.
Accessories = Options!

Shopping . . .

Wherever, Whenever!

Sometimes it's fun to hit the stores and pick out things in person.

Other times, it's even better to sit in front of your computer and say, "No, I believe I'll let Mr. Postman deliver these items to me."

Web sites to Fulfill Shopping Fantasies

WEB SITE: _____

A GO-TO PLACE FOR:

_____

WEB SITE: _____

A GO-TO PLACE FOR:

_____

* Diva Pointer: Remember that you can still make an event of your online shopping! Put on your comfiest house slippers, turn on some music or a beloved TV show, get yourself a nice drink, and cuddle up to your computer.

Shopping for . . .

A Deal

Know what's almost as incredible
as releasing your inner diva?
Releasing your inner bargainista!

When you find deals, you save money . . .
and then you can splurge on even more!

Diva Discount Discovery Tips

1. Type into your Web browser the name of your favorite store and the words "coupon code" or "promo code." You may find lots of discounts you wouldn't know about otherwise!

2. Go to your favorite stores' Web sites to learn about coupons, sales, and upcoming promotions.

3. Look for coupons the old-fashioned way: in newspapers.

4. Ask if your favorite store has a rewards or membership program for frequent shoppers.

5. If you're flexible about where you buy things, visit an online auction site. Oftentimes you can get exactly what you want for a significantly lower price!

"Yeah, yeah, yeah," you may be saying. "Clothes, shoes, and accessories are fine—but they aren't what I like to splurge on."

So what's your thing?
Getting down with your "inner diva" doesn't
have to be about shopping for your wardrobe.

Shopping for . . .
Your Life

**Maybe you pick out something that speaks to you,
your life, and your interests.**

. . . .

Love interior decorating?
Go for that vase or frame you'd usually pass up.

All about cooking or baking?
Treat yourself to some gourmet kitchen supplies.

Proud of your car?
You might be in for some new floor mats!

It's your shopping spree, and you'll spend how you want to!

Shopping for . . .

Your Entertainment

Delight your eyes and ears by
splurging on something entertaining.

What will you choose?

- Rent a movie

- Go out to a movie

- Download a song (or two or three . . .)

- Download a game, TV show, or other digital delight

- Invest in new reading material

Shopping for . . .

Your Inner Gadget Gal

Do you appreciate the value of cool phones, TVs, cameras, MP3 players, and other electronic gizmos?

Then embrace your "wired" side!

✳ **Diva Pointer**: When you've got some funds to spare, you can always put a "diva" spin on your electronics shopping. Get a trendy laptop bag, a fashionable case for your phone, or an MP3 player in a fun, funky color.

Shopping . . .

Some Time for You

. . . .

Here's the thing:

Knowing you, it's easy to guess that you
probably wouldn't get all "diva" on your own.

(You're waaaay too nice for that.)

So that's why you're getting this little
bit of encouragement.

Because you totally deserve to splurge
on something that's as fabulous as you are.

Use this to have an amazing time picking out exactly what you want!

**INSERT MONEY
OR GIFT CARD HERE**

$ _____